$+$ $=$ 10 $\div$ IV

1 $\frac{1}{2}$

3 5

101
Ways to
Boost
Your
Math
Skills

$\div$ 6

$\frac{1}{4}$ 3

1 V

V 2

5 V $=$ 7 8

Susan Shafer

Troll Associates

To Ron

Text and illustrations copyright © 1996 by Troll Communications L.L.C.

Published by Troll Associates, an imprint and registered trademark
of Troll Communications L.L.C.

Printed in the United States of America.

10 9 8 7 6 5 4 3 2 1

ACKNOWLEDGMENTS

My thanks to Dr. Marianne Tully, principal of the William O. Schaefer Elementary School in the South Orangetown Central School District, in Tappan, New York. Marianne's enthusiasm and energy for teaching and learning are clearly contagious. Thanks, too, to Bob Hendrickson, principal of the Cottage Lane School, and Emmanuel Kostakis, principal of the South Orangetown Middle School in Blauvelt, New York.

Special thanks to Suzanne Mantin and Kathleen Lacker, math teachers in South Orangetown Central Middle School, and to Valerie Malkus, 4th grade teacher at the Cottage Lane School. They clearly love their work.

I certainly appreciate the suggestions offered by these students: Joey Ameen, Chris Annunziato, Alberto Bariffi, Megan Blossom, Cecelia Cabrera, Chris Campon, Edel Carolan, Charmae Carter, Gina Cassese, Tobin Chacko, Daniel Chan, Peter Chand, Michael Chu, Jennifer Chu, Cattleya Concepcion, Caitlin Coulch, Kristen DeMaria, Colin Desuro, Martina Fox, Nina Glaser, Jose Guerrero, Crystal Hrynenko, Melissa Huberfeld, Stephen Hueg, Christine Kim, Michelle Kim, Patricia MacKinzee, Nell Macy, Marcella Mazzeo, Ashley McCarthy, Maria Mirakoj, Chris Mooney, Jennifer Nath, Marisela Navas, Caitlin Nugent, Samantha Orenstein, Catherine O'Sullivan, Jon Oy, Lijo G. Padannamacral, Christina Park, Jeannie Park, Cynthia Phillips, Andrew Robert-Louche, Alexis Roosa, David Rosenberg, Rachel Roth, Scottie Salamon, Anwar Sawyer, Mark Serrete, Ariana Skakieh, Gregory Soyk, John Tan, Kerri Trendowicz, Emily Treubig, Suzzie Uy, Paul Vasquez-Negron, Paul Vellucci, Rebecca Vogel, and Geoffrey Whelan.

I'm grateful to Eileen Erickson, communications manager, National Council of Teachers of Mathematics, for putting me in touch with a number of talented math teachers throughout the country, including Jenny Rodriquez of Visalia, California. Thanks also goes to David S. Badger, executive director of the Beacon Day School in Oakland, California.

Contents

CHAPTER 1

Math Is Everywhere!

When you think of math, what "pictures" come to mind. Your math teacher? Your math book? Multiplication tables? Subtraction examples? These are all good answers, but did you know that math is more than math class and homework assignments? Though you may not be aware of it, math is as much a part of your life as eating or sleeping.

How could that be? Imagine this: You're running around your house one morning, packing your bookbag, afraid that you'll be late for school. Dashing through the kitchen, you glance at the clock on the wall. "Oh, no. It's 7:50 a.m.!" you shout. "I'll be late for the bus!" (Hint: Telling time is math!) Now you're frantically searching for lunch money. You pluck five quarters, a dime, and a nickel from a pile of change on the counter. "Ma, I took $1.40 for lunch money," you shout. (Hint: Dealing with money is math, too.) Think about the rest of your week. Do you get an allowance? Earn money at an afterschool or weekend job? Check a map for the distance form your house to a vaction spot? Figure out the number of pizza slices coming to each hungry person at the table? (Hint: Dividing eight slices by four people is doing math.)

We could go on and on. The point is that all of these everyday activities involve a knowledge of math. Math is time and money. And logic. And geometry and shapes, and fractions, and reasoning. In short, math is everywhere!

This is how one student said it:

"Math is good to know because if you didn't have numbers you wouldn't know how much things cost. If you're in a car, you wouldn't know how fast you're going or what exit to get off. You would never know what time it is, or how many books are in a collection. You would never know how many letters there are in the alphabet."

Why Read This Book?

You deserve to be congratulated. By selecting *101 Ways to Boost Your Math Skills* you've taken a first step toward shining in math—in school or outside. Sure, you want to raise your grades. Who wouldn't? This book can help by giving tips on improving your work habits, your study skills, and your homework. (Won't your parents and teachers be thrilled!) Plus, it gives sound advice for improving your scores on those all-important math tests. No matter what your grades, you can become faster, more confident, more enthusiastic, and more flexible in math every day by following some of our suggestions.

Of course, you don't have to read every page. You can look at the Contents page and pick the chapter that interests you the most. Or if you like, you can read the book cover to cover, tackling a chapter a day. Whatever your approach, you can sharpen your math skills in small or big ways.

Most of the suggestions here were given by grownups. But we know that other kids can give valuable advice as well. That's why we asked some middle school students to offer tips. You'll find their ideas in the next chapter and in boxes labeled "Student to Student" throughout the book.

Good luck, and read on! You can do it!

CHAPTER 2

Advice from the Experts: Other Kids

We asked some good math students for tips on how to do well in math. Here is what they said.

? WHAT IS MATH?

"Math is a skill. It is not about being able to multiply, divide, and **A** so on, but about knowing *when* to multiply or divide. If you are good at multiplying, but you don't know *when* to multiply, there is no use knowing how. Math is about knowing when to do something."

"Math is more than just subtraction and addition. It is shapes and sizes and money. It is your life. Think about what the world would be like without math and numbers."

? WHAT'S THE KEY TO SUCCESS?

"If you don't like how you're doing in math, keep trying. Don't get discouraged or you may do just the opposite of what you want."

"If there's a Math Club or Team in your school, join it. It will help you understand math and enjoy it. Joining a club or team can help you get ahead. You never know, math just might be your major in college."

? HOW CAN YOU ACE A MATH TEST?

"When you study at night, it is always best to review your work in the morning to refresh your memory. You can review it when you're eating your breakfast. It really does help!"

"Don't panic beforehand and try to do your best."

? WHAT IF YOU DO POORLY ON A TEST?

A "If you get a bad mark, tell your parents that you tried your best and that you will try harder next time. If you think you need help, ask for it or stay after school for a while."

? WHAT IF YOU'RE CONFUSED?

A "It really helps to ask a teacher, friend, or parent for help. Sometimes when there is no one to ask, you just have to keep trying until you can achieve your goal. Math might not be what you're best at, but you still need it in your life."

CHAPTER 3

Getting to Know Yourself

1. **SEARCH FOR YOUR SKILLS.** The secret to boosting your math skills is to know three things about yourself:
- Your strengths—what you're already good at
- Your needs—where you can use some help
- Your goals—how you want to improve, and by when

Start by filling in the *My Math Profile* on pages 16-19 of this book. When you're finished, read over what you've written and think about what you've learned about yourself. (Take your time. These are not one word answers.) If you like, talk about your answers with a family member or a friend.

2. **WHAT'S YOUR GOAL?** Reread your answers to n. and o. on the *My Math Profile* form. Pick a goal and write it on one of the coupons on pages 20 and 21. Tape it above your desk. When you've reached that goal, pick a new one. Says a happy sixth grader, "My brother couldn't figure out what those math coupons were on my desk. But when my math grades went up, he started staring at them and saying, 'Cool!'."

My Math Profile

Make a photocopy of these pages or rewrite them in a notebook or on a computer.

Take your time as you fill in the answers. They will tell you a lot about your feelings and math skills. The questions may even bring out some feelings about math you didn't know you had! When you're finished, read over your responses. What have you learned about yourself?

a. Do you like math? Why or why not?

_____

_____

b. In what ways do you use math outside of school?

_____

_____

c. Why do you think it might be useful to boost your math skills?

_____

_____

d. How do you feel about math class?

_____

_____

e. What are your favorite topics in math? Put a check.
   What are your least favorite topics? Put an X.

   ☐ geometry   ☐ division
   ☐ measurement   ☐ problem solving
   ☐ decimals   ☐ probability and statistics
   ☐ fractions   ☐ algebra
   ☐ multiplication   ☐ solving equations
   ☐ subtraction   ☐ graphs
   ☐ addition

f. How would your teacher describe your math skills?
   (You can ask your teacher if you're not sure.)

   _____

   _____

g. What does your report card say about your math
   skills?

   _____

   _____

h. What does your mom or dad say about your math
   skills?

   _____

   _____

i. In what areas of math are you strongest (for example, addition or problem solving)?

_____

_____

j. In what areas of math are you weakest (for example, division or fractions)?

_____

_____

k. What have you learned in math class so far this year?

_____

_____

l. What do you do when you're stuck on a math problem in class?

_____

_____

m. What do you do when you're stuck on a math problem at home?

_____

_____

n. In what areas of math do you hope to improve?

_____

_____

o. What are your goals for improving your math skills over the next week?

_____

_____

p. What are your goals for improving your math skills by the next marking period?

_____

_____

Congratulations!

You've already taken the first steps toward sharpening your math skills!

My Math Goals

When you decide on a goal, fill in one of the coupons, cut it out, and tape it on the desk or table where you study. When you've reached that goal, throw out the paper and fill in a new one.

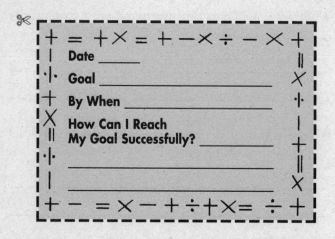

Date _____
Goal _____
By When _____
How Can I Reach
My Goal Successfully? _____
_____
_____

Date _____
Goal _____
By When _____
How Can I Reach
My Goal Successfully? _____
_____
_____

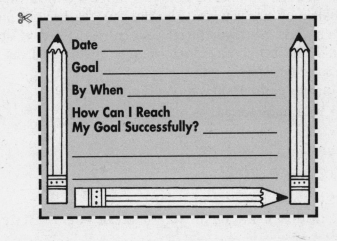

Date _____

Goal _____

By When _____

How Can I Reach
My Goal Successfully? _____

_____

_____

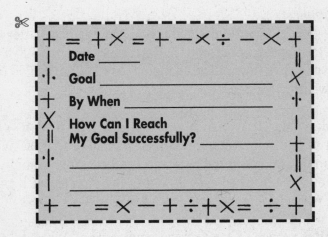

Date _____

Goal _____

By When _____

How Can I Reach
My Goal Successfully? _____

_____

_____

21

3. **KEEP A MATH JOURNAL.** Using a notebook, diary, or loose-leaf book, write down your thoughts and feelings about math every day, or at the very least, once a week. Writing in a journal will help you notice the kinds of math situations where you get tense—or have fun. Use your journal to describe how you solved a difficult math problem or how you reacted when your teacher called on you in class. When you reread your entries a few days later, you'll find better ways to solve your math problems or reasons to celebrate your successes!

In your journal you can reflect on:
- your math teacher
- your math assignments
- your math tests
- special math projects
- the kids in math class
- math at home, on the way to school, or at the store

Examples:

Tuesday: "Today Mom asked me to give the baby-sitter her pay for the day, which is $42. Mom gave me three $20 bills. I wasn't sure how much change to ask for, but Jackie (the baby-sitter) helped."

Friday: "Mr. Bickworth is so-o-o-o-o strict! Today he gave us a two-minute test on fractions. We had to see how many examples we could finish before the bell rang. Would you believe it? I finished only 29 out of 50! Monday we'll try it again. My goal is to get at least 40 right!"

After a week or two, reread your journal. What did you discover about yourself?

4. **ME AT MY BEST.** Do you shake when your math teacher calls on you in class? Do you put off doing your math homework for as long as possible? If so, you may have math anxiety. That means you get so tense about math that you can't enjoy it at all. (Believe it or not, math can be lots of fun!)

One way to solve this problem is to create a Math Success Notebook. This is like a journal, but in it you record only good experiences you've had with math. Did you get a 100% on today's math quiz? Did you figure out your correct change at the grocery store? Write those down. A Math Success Notebook will help build your confidence and convince you that your skills are stronger than you think!

> October 6:
>
> Awesome! Went to computer
> store with Dad. Figured out
> 10% discount on $39.99
> CD-ROM package fast
> (in my head) by checking
> out the first two digits of
> the original price (approximate
> discount = $3.90).
>
> No paper or pencil needed!

CHAPTER 4

You and Your Work Habits

5. **CUT THE CLUTTER.** Keep all the things on your desk neat and organized. Put pencils in a cup or pencil holder. Store pads of paper in a drawer or in a tidy pile. Keep the pencil sharpener in a special spot. You should not have to waste time searching for stuff each time you go to your desk. Your tools and materials should always be in the same place.

6. **FOCUS.** Are you easily distracted? If so, try to find a quieter work place. Does your desk face a window from which you can watch kids playing outside? Move your desk against the wall instead. Does the chatter of the TV make you lose your concentration? Ask a family member to turn it down.

7. **YOU'RE IN CHARGE.** Remember—you're the one who is responsible for your math learning. Your parents can help, and so can your teacher. But it's your job, not someone else's, to improve your math. Take charge of your own learning!

8. **PAT YOURSELF ON THE BACK.** When you're feeling down, remind yourself of all you know in math.

In just a few short years, you've learned how to add, subtract, multiply, and divide, right? What else can you do in math? Every few weeks, make a list. You may be surprised at all you know.

9. **TIME IS OF THE ESSENCE!** Pick a time every day when you can do your math homework. This may be right after school (say, 4 p.m. every day), or before your favorite TV shows (say, weekdays from 7 p.m. to 8 p.m.). Make sure it's a time when you feel relaxed and you know you can concentrate. Then stick to that schedule.

10. **DISPLAY YOUR OFFICE HOURS.** Post your daily math study schedule in a prominent place over your desk. If a family member interrupts you, point to your schedule and politely say, "This is my math study time. Can we talk later?"

11. **REWARD YOURSELF.** Do you love in-line skating? Thin pretzels? Computer games? Think of a great reward that will motivate you to work hard. Write it down on a piece of paper and post it over your desk. ("My reward: Play my new CD-ROM for ten minutes today.") When you've met your math goal for the day, give yourself that treat. You deserve it!

12. **WELCOME TO MATH PLACE.** Organize your notebook into subject areas, such as Math, Social Studies, and Science. For the Math section, make a pocket for storing all your important math papers, tests, and letters home. Cut a piece of colored poster paper to the same width as your notebook and half the height. Staple the two sides and the bottom of your pocket to the first page of the

Math section in your notebook. Leave the pocket top open to store your materials. Clean out and organize the papers every week.

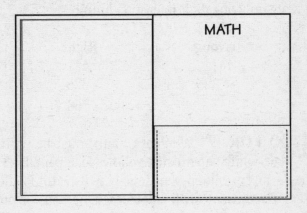

13. **SQUIGGLES WON'T HELP.** Want to improve the looks of your homework? If you cram all the numbers into a small corner, they'll be hard to read. Leave plenty of "air" between numbers and between examples, too. This way, your teacher will be able to read your handwriting, and you'll be less likely to make mistakes.

14. **MAKE MATH FUN.** Convince yourself that math homework is fun, fun, fun! If this doesn't come naturally, find ways to make it enjoyable. Buy scratch paper with funny cartoons around the border. Tape humorous messages around your desk, bulletin board, or computer screen. Let these relax you. As you start a math assignment, adopt a playful, gamelike attitude. You may actually enjoy yourself!

15. **WHAT A MESS!** If you're doing a page filled with numbers, make sure the columns line up correctly. The tens should all be in the tens column and the ones in the ones column. If necessary, fold your paper into columns and write only one digit in each column.

Wrong	Right
441	441
+ 325	+325
	766

16. **GO FOR IT!** Who says math must be written on plain white paper using yellow No. 2 pencils? To perk yourself up, try wild, psychedelic pencils with doodle-head erasers. Experiment with colorful felt-tip pens or hot pink or lime green notepads. Use tools that scream "This is Great!"

17. **TALK IT OUT.** "My dad was always comparing me to my older brother—the 'Math Genius,'" says Betty, a sixth grader. "It made me freeze up in math class and I felt I couldn't do anything right. But we talked it over at our family meeting Sunday night, and I got it off my chest." Are you anxious about math? How did that awful feeling get started in your mind? Consider what's making you tense, then talk it through with someone you trust. Sharing your problem is half the battle in conquering it.

18. **SHHH!** If it's simply too noisy to study in your house, ask your parents for permission to study at the local library. (Call your branch for its hours.) There you can find a quiet table, maybe even a study center, for the most privacy. While you're at the library, apply for a library card (if you don't already have one) and check out some of the math books listed on pages 89-91 of *101 Ways to Boost Your Math Skills*.

19. **STRUCTURE YOUR NOTES.** As your teacher walks you through the lesson on the chalkboard in class, take notes on a double-column page of your notebook. Review the notes when you get home. The numbers and the reasons for each step will make more sense. On the left side of the page, write the steps in the example. On the right side, write the explanation for each step. Like this:

3,5 28 ②47 <u>5,2 51</u>	Find the smallest addend. Circle its first digit
3 5 28 2 47 5 2 51	Circle all the digits in that column.
(3,500) 200 <u>5,300</u>	Round off all the numbers.
3,500 200 <u>5,300</u> 9,000	Add to find the sum.

CHAPTER 5

You and Your Study Skills

20. **WHAT'S TO GAIN?** Convince yourself that studying math is cool. Remind yourself of all its benefits. (For example: You'll become an A+ student. Your parents will be proud of you when you bring home an excellent report card. Other kids will admire you.)

21. **M IS FOR MNEMONICS.** "Chord." "Mode." "Diameter." What's a nifty way to remember these hard math words and what they mean? Think of something you associate with the term, such as a rhyming word or an object that reminds you of it. This is called using a mnemonic device. Mnemonic devices aid the memory.

Suppose you read in your math textbook that a chord is a line segment whose endpoints are on the outer edge of a circle.

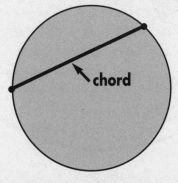

Think of a way—even a silly one—to remind yourself of the word's meaning.

"Let's see," you might say to yourself, "a *cord* (spelled differently from *chord*) is a piece of rope that, when pulled tight, might make a straight line. A person might hold on to a cord to cross a lake. Even though the words only sound the same, every time I read *chord* I'll think of *cord*. I'll picture a person grasping a cord to get across a circular lake. That will remind me that a chord is a line segment across a circle."

22. **POST IT.** If you've learned many formulas in class, make a master list of them and tape them to your desk for easy reference. Review them daily.

FORMULAS

Length x Width x
Height = Volume

Pi = 3.14

Length x Width =
Area of a Rectangle

23. **DOES THIS MAKE SENSE?** When you've finished a problem, consider if the answer makes sense. Suppose you're doing a large multiplication example. Your answer is smaller than the number with which you started. Does that make sense? Hardly! Review your work to see where you went off track.

24. LOOK FOR A PATTERN. If you can spot a pattern in a chart or diagram, you may be able to find the solution to the question quickly. A pattern is something that repeats itself. Study this chart. It shows how much Ralph got paid every day. Every day he gets a raise. How much will Ralph earn on 1/10?

Date	Earned
1/6	$2.00
1/7	$2.25
1/8	$2.50
1/9	$2.75
1/10	_____

Note the pattern. His pay increased by 25 cents every day. Therefore, he will earn $3.00 on 1/10.

25. WHERE WAS I? Before you begin studying, take a few minutes to review what you learned yesterday. This will put you in the right frame of mind for today's lesson. At the end of your study session, spend a minute summarizing what you learned.

26. **ASK MOM OR DAD.** Was your mom or dad an above-average math student as a kid? If so, ask your parent what he or she did to succeed in math. Did she memorize math facts by singing them out loud in her bedroom every night? Did he recite his multiplication tables into an audiotape, then check them later? Find out your parent's tricks, and adopt them for yourself.

27. **LISTEN UP.** After you've read through a math problem, try teaching it to someone else. Explain what you're going to teach, then go over all the steps, giving reasons for each. You can call a friend on the phone, or call a parent at work. If you can explain it, you probably understand it.

28. **GIVE IT TIME.** Learning math does not always happen overnight. Give yourself permission to let a math problem sink in. Don't expect to understand it that day. Give yourself a few days to get it.

29. **KNOCK, KNOCK.** Start your study session by reading a few math jokes aloud, such as those compiled by Charles Keller in *Take Me to Your Liter: Science and Math Jokes* (Pippin Press, 1991). These will relax you and put you in a let's-have-some-math-fun frame of mind.

30. **HOMEWORK HELPER.** Do you dislike math homework? Some kids do. That's because they don't understand the reasons for it. Remind yourself that homework is assigned to give you practice at learning a new skill. When you practice a skill, it starts to become automatic, even fun. The next time you have a homework assignment, think of all the good things that it can do for you!

31. **BE PERSISTENT.** If you're working on a tough assignment, don't give up. Keep plugging away at it, and before you know it, you'll have the answer.

32. **WHO'S THE BEST?** Start your study sessions with an I-Am-Wonderful chant. In your head, or mumbling, tell yourself how great you are in math. Build your confidence. Convince yourself that you're the tops!

One fifth grader began her work sessions like this: "I am an excellent math student. My intelligence knows no bounds. I can do math feats known to few others. My teacher thinks I'm the best math student she's ever had in her entire teaching career. I happen to agree with her. I'm great at . . ."

33. **MUSIC MAGIC.** Who is your favorite recording artist? If it won't distract you, play some background music as you study. Let it soothe you as you work.

34. **FULL OF BEANS!** Do you hate to memorize multiplication facts? Do you find them boring or tedious? There's an easy solution! Grab a friend or a brother or sister and a bag filled with beans.

MAKE A BEAN BAG

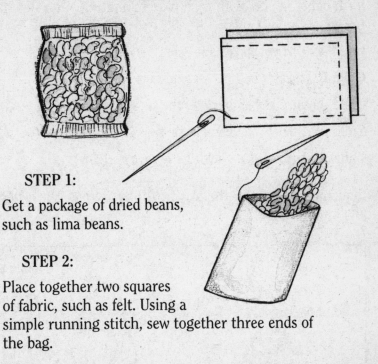

STEP 1:

Get a package of dried beans,
such as lima beans.

STEP 2:

Place together two squares
of fabric, such as felt. Using a
simple running stitch, sew together three ends of
the bag.

STEP 3:

Turn the bag inside out. Fill it with beans, and sew up
the fourth side.

STEP 4:

Use the bean bag to play Multiplication Toss.

How to Play: For each math fact, toss the bag back and forth between you, with each player shouting out a step of the equation, like this:

Child A: (throws bag as she says . . .) 4

Child B: (throws bag back as he says . . .) times

Child A: (throws bag back as she says . . .) 6

Child A: (throws bag back as he says . . .) equals

Child B: (throws bag back as she says . . .) 24

Remember, the faster the players throw the bag, the faster you must respond!

35. **ROCK 'N ROLL MATH.** Invest in some lively rock or rap math audiotapes that help you practice your addition, subtraction, multiplication, and division. Some tapes even come packaged with books of games, puzzles, and mazes to give you quick recall of facts.

CHAPTER 6

You and Your Teacher

36. MATH IS MORE THAN TESTS. Teachers base kids' grades on more than just test scores. Many math teachers value neatness, interest in the subject, and punctuality in arriving to class. Do you hand in homework with your numbers and letters neatly formed? Are your papers unwrinkled and free of stains, such as spaghetti sauce or ketchup? Do you appear interested in class? Show up on time? Ask questions? Teachers think of these things when composing your grade. You should, too.

37. GIVE NOTICES TO PARENTS. Teachers urge parents to show up for Parent/Teacher Night or Open School Week for very good reasons. They want to share with parents how the students are progressing. During these important meetings, your teacher and your parent can find ways to help you raise those grades. Make sure you give your parents the newsletters, announcements, and other invitations to these special events. Mark these days on the family calendar with large capital letters in zany colors.

38. **WAIT UP!** If your math teacher is talking too fast during a lesson and you are unable to follow the steps, raise your hand and politely ask him or her to speak more slowly. It's a simple and reasonable request.

39. **MAKE YOUR CHALLENGES KNOWN.** Do you have special needs, such as a hearing weakness or poor eyesight? Make sure your math teacher is aware of this. Your teacher can sit you near the front of the room, where you can catch every word and see the chalkboard more clearly.

40. **DON'T GET DISCOURAGED.** Sure, sometimes the lessons may seem difficult. You may not feel sure of yourself at all times. But the payoffs—getting good grades, learning useful techniques, graduating with honors—will be rewarding in the end. Hang in there! Take a chance.

41. **TEACHERS ARE HUMAN.** It's easy to learn a subject from a person you like or respect. Keep in mind that your teacher has interests outside the classroom. Try to find out what these are. Does your teacher like football? Computer games? Travel? Knowing your teacher's likes and dislikes can help you feel closer to him or her and more relaxed in class.

42. **GO THE EXTRA MILE.** You can boost your math skills by taking on special projects. Before or after class, ask your teacher if there are special drills or activities you can do—apart from your regular homework—that will strengthen your skills. Start a math newsletter for kids? Demonstrate how to balance a checkbook? Report on statistics for your favorite baseball team? Ask your teacher to suggest a project, or better yet, come up with an idea of your own. Be creative!

43. **CHECK OUT YOUR TEACHER'S LIBRARY.** Many math teachers have interesting books on their subject. One book, *The Math Teacher's Book of Lists* by Judith A. Muschla and Gary R. Muschla (Prentice Hall, 1995), contains fascinating information, from the odds of winning various games to famous mathematicians in history. Ask your teacher if you can borrow or browse through these books. They will surely inspire you—and your teacher will be impressed!

CHAPTER 7

Tricks of the Trade

44. **ESTIMATE FIRST!** Before you actually work out a math problem, first guess what the answer will be. That way, when you do your calculations, you'll know if your answer is way off base. You could try again.

For example, let's say you're asked to find the distance a car traveled if it went 54 miles an hour for 16 hours. You know the formula: Rate x Time = Distance.

Before you do the actual computing, estimate. ("Let's see. If I round off the 54 to 50, and the 16 to 20, then multiply 50 times 20, I get an estimate of 1,000 miles.") When you do the actual example, you'll know if your answer is about right. (Actual answer? 864 miles)

STUDENT TO STUDENT:

"I think you should always use 'Lazy Loops' when multiplying by one hundred. All you have to do is move the decimal point over two places to the right. This is where lazy loops come in handy. You can draw a loop from the place where the decimal is to two places to the right. It saves the time of multiplying it out."

$$7.589 \times 100 = 758.9$$

45. DIAGRAM IT!

If you're working on a big problem with lots of possible answers, organize them into a Venn diagram. You don't have to hold all the answers "in your head."

Example:

You're taking a survey of your classmates' favorite foods. (They can pick more than one.) After you poll each student, organize the answers on a diagram so you can "see" the answers clearly and add the numbers in each category. Display your diagram to the class as part of your report.

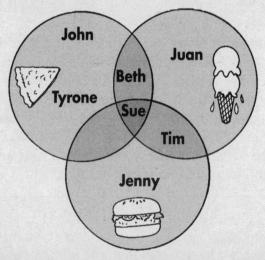

STUDENT TO STUDENT:

"When you are doing a word problem and you don't know whether to add, subtract, multiply, or divide, look for the words 'in all' in the problem. If they're there, you would add, because 'in all' means add up everything you have."

46. GET THE PICTURE?

As often as possible, draw a picture or diagram to help you visualize and solve a problem. What if the teacher asked you to find the perimeter of the schoolyard, which is 50 feet long and 20 feet wide? First, make a quick sketch to help you picture the scene in your mind. Then add all four sides to find the perimeter.

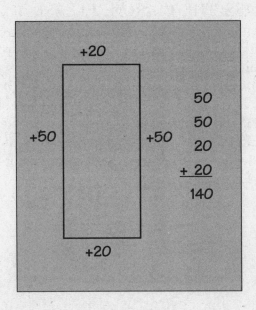

Get the picture?

47. **PAGE TURNERS.** Read lots of books with math challenges. For example, Bill Brittain's *All the Money in the World* and Marilyn Burns' The *I Hate Mathematics! Book* pose some interesting questions that will test your skills in math reasoning and problem solving. Read the books to younger children and help them figure out the answers.

48. **PASS THE CD-ROM, PLEASE.** If you have a computer or access to someone else's, invest in math practice CD-ROMs especially designed to help you practice your skills, from problem solving to fractions. Visit your local software store and browse until you find the right one for your age and needs. Or find out if your local library has CD-ROMS you can borrow. You may even be able to use the CD-ROMS at the library's computer center. If you don't know how to use CD-ROMS, ask the librarian if the library sponsors classes.

STUDENT TO STUDENT:

"When my teacher taught me about estimating, I said, 'Why do I have to estimate when I could just figure out the answer without it?' Then I realized that it is easier to estimate. If you need to practice estimating, do it with your mom's grocery list, so she knows how much she needs before going shopping."

Example:

vitamins	$4.50
roast beef	$10.25
cereal	$3.57
toothpaste	$2.98

"You can say, '$4.50 can stay as that and so can $10.25. That adds up to $14.75. $3.57 can round off to $4.00 and $2.98 rounds off to $3.00. If I add that up I get $21.75.' Your mom can take that amount out of her purse. So you're not only practicing estimating, you're helping your mom."

CHAPTER 8

I'm Stuck!
Solving Problems

49. **IT WAS THERE ALL ALONG!** Sometimes when you're trying to solve a math problem, you may force yourself to keep working at it until you find the solution. This may not be as helpful as you think.

If you get stuck on an example, put it aside for a while. Take a five-minute break. (Play with the cat! Get a snack!) Do something completely different that will get your mind on something else. When you feel refreshed, go back to the problem and read it with a fresh eye. Suddenly you may see the solution!

STUDENT TO STUDENT:

"If you have a subtraction problem that you don't understand, start at the smaller number and count up until you get to the higher number. See how many numbers it takes to get to the higher number. That's your answer. *Example:* 8 – 3 = ? Start at 3. Think 4 (that's one number), 5 (that's another number), 6 (that's another number), 7 (that's another number), and 8 (that's the last number). You counted 5 numbers in all. The answer to 8 – 3 is 5!"

---

50. **THINK ALOUD.** Do word problems have you down? We've got a solution: Hold a "think-aloud." Say the problem as you work it out on paper. This may help you "hear" errors in your reasoning.

Pretend you've read this example in your math book: On their vacation, the Johnsons spent $150 for food the first day, $200 the second day, and $155 the third day. How much did the Johnsons spend on average for food on that trip?

Think aloud: "Let's see, I'm asked to find an average. I know that to find an average I add up the numbers and divide by that many elements. I'll do the calculation.

"Adding up $150, $200, and $155, I get $405. Oops, I added wrong. It's really $505. Now I divide $505 by 3, which equals $168.33. Now I'll go back and check my answer."

51. TRY ANOTHER WAY.

Imagine that you're walking home from school. Your usual route is to walk one block east on Sunset and two blocks north on Franklin to your home on Amsterdam. As you approach Franklin Street one afternoon, you discover that the road is blocked off by construction equipment. What would you do? You'd probably backtrack on Sunset, walking west to find a different street (perhaps Columbus, which is parallel to Franklin) leading to your house. The same method of finding alternative solutions can be used for tackling math problems. Let's say you've attempted to solve a difficult example, but you're not getting anywhere with it. What can you do? Try another path. Don't give up. There are usually many possible avenues to success.

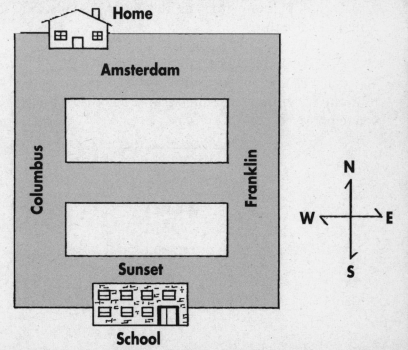

52. WE'RE RELATED.

If you're handed a tough problem, try creating a new, simpler problem that is like the original one, but is easier to solve.

Let's say you are asked to do this division example with decimals:

$$85.20 \,\, \overline{)305.016}$$

Make it simpler by dropping the decimal points. Now you must solve this:

$$8520 \,\, \overline{)305016}$$

You find that the answer is 358. Go back to the harder problem, figure out where the decimal point belongs, and you're home free!

```
                 3.58
      8520 √ 305016 0
           25560
           49416
           42600
            6816 0
```

53. **HELP IS ON THE WAY!** If you need extra help, ask your mom or dad to hire you a math tutor. A tutor is an instructor who will give you special help. The tutor may give you practice in math facts and may help you solve math problems. Math tutors can be math teachers, college students, or honor students in your school. Some get paid by the hour, while others tutor for free. One fourth grader worked with a private tutor for only two months and her math scores shot up. By the next marking period, she no longer needed the tutor.

STUDENT TO STUDENT:
"Math is not only numbers and rules, but shapes and blocks and geometry. There are many ways to learn math."

ACT IT OUT!
Sometimes it helps to actually walk through the steps to a problem. And we do mean walk! Let's say you're trying to solve a perimeter question. You need to find the perimeter of a schoolyard 110 feet long by 60 feet wide. Try taking ministeps around your room, each step representing ten feet. Add as you go. Before long you'll have the answer (and a bit of exercise).

54. **GET REAL!** Some problems will become clearer if you use concrete objects to help you picture them. Find items from around your room, such as bottle caps, buttons, paper clips, or thumb tacks, to make a problem come alive.

55. **WHAT'S THE PROBLEM?** In your own words, restate the problem. ("They want me to find out how much Timmy will earn by Christmas. He starts his job in September at $3,000 and he gets a raise of $400 at the beginning of each new month.") Do you understand the problem now? Rephrasing the problem will help you focus on what's really being asked.

56. **SET UP A PROPORTION.** Some word problems can be expressed as a ratio or proportion. A *ratio* is a comparison of two quantities. When you compare two ratios, you have a *proportion*.

Example:

Mr. Hopper sells magazines at his table at the flea market. He offers them at 4 for $1. How many magazines can a customer buy for $5?

WHAT TO DO: Think, "If four magazines sell for $1, how many can be bought with $5? I'll write that as a ratio."

Set up the ratio as a fraction.

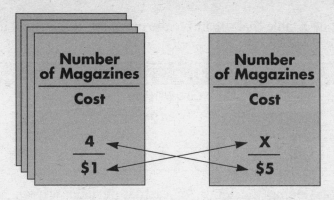

Now cross-multiply the numerators and denominators of the fractions to find the answer.

$$1x = 20$$
$$x = 20$$

For $5, a customer can buy 20 magazines.

57. CHART YOUR COURSE. Word problems often contain lots of information, too much to really hold in your head at one time. Organize the information in a more readable form, such as a table or a chart.

Example:
You read this problem:

In February, the Alpha Video store rented out 125 videos for grownups and 55 for kids. Across the street, the Beta Video store rented 85 videos for grownups and 65 for kids. Around the block, Delta Videos rented 210 videos for grownups and 55 for kids. Which store sold the most videos (grownups and kids combined)?

Set up a table that organizes the numbers. It may look like this.

VIDEOS SOLD		
Store	Grownups	Kids
Alpha	12	55
Beta	5	65
Delta	85	55

By finding the totals for each store (add across), you quickly see that the Delta Video Store sold the most videos—265.

58. WORK BACKWARD. Some problems are best solved by working backward, not forward. You decide whether to use this strategy depending on the nature of the problem. You can even draw a picture to make it clearer.

Example:
Three rabbits were in a race to see who could hop the farthest in a given time. Belinda Rabbit hopped 3 yards farther than Petunia Rabbit. Amelia Rabbit was the winner; she jumped 10 yards in all, which was 3 yards more than Belinda. How many yards did Petunia jump?

Work this problem backward. Amelia jumped the farthest, which was 10 yards. (Start with 10.) Amelia jumped 3 yards more than Belinda. (To find how far Belinda jumped, subtract 3 from 10. That's 7 yards.) We know that Petunia jumped 3 yards less than Belinda. (7 minus 3 is 4.)

Answer: Petunia jumped 4 yards.

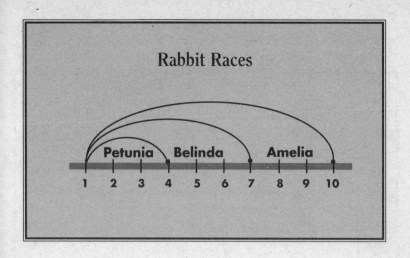

CHAPTER 9

Special Projects:
On Your Own

59. BUY OR SELL? Do you know what the stock market is? It's a way to invest your money in big and small companies by buying their "stock," which represents a bit of ownership of the business. If you buy stock in a company and the price goes up, you make money. If the price goes down, you lose money. It can be very risky. (No place to put your allowance!) But many people make money this way.

Using just a newspaper and paper and pencil, you can invest in the market with no risk at all! Pretend to buy and sell stocks, keeping track of your gains and losses. A fifth grader who did this said, "At first I was glad I invested in that stock. In only one month I made a $400 profit. But I didn't sell soon enough. By the next month my stock went down. If I had invested for real, I would have lost my principal." (*Principal* means initial investment.)

Get a newspaper that lists the stocks. Ask a parent to explain what the numbers mean. Follow your stocks and see how much you make or lose each week.

60. COUNT YOUR MONEY.

Do you get an allowance? Do you earn money in your spare time? If so, you can use that money to teach yourself math.

Open your bank. How much money have you saved? Count your stash in as many ways as possible: by ones, by twos, by fives. Now do some mental math. If your money doubles in a month, how much will you have then? In three months? In a year?

What if you put your money in the bank? The bank offers a 3% interest rate. How much money will you have next year?

Try to think flexibly. It's the key to math success.

61. **NEXT TELLER, PLEASE.** Speaking of money, you should open a bank account of your own. Some banks allow this, as long as a parent or guardian co-signs. This means that your parent or guardian would be responsible for your account, too. Check with your bank to see if it allows this. If so, the initial deposit may be quite small, perhaps only $5.

Think this over: What is the current interest rate? If you open a bank account today, how much money will you make in a month? In six months? What is the rate of inflation? Is your money keeping up with inflation? Why or why not? Figure these questions out, working with a parent or a bank employee, if possible.

62. **SKILL DRILL.** Have you ever used math flash cards in school? If so, you know the cards contain basic math you need to know automatically, such as multiplication and division facts. The question is usually written on the front, and the answer, used for checking, is printed on the back. Memorizing these facts can save you a lot of time.

Pick an area in which you need help (fractions, for example). Ask your parents to buy you a pack of flash cards, or make your own using index cards. Practice with them for five minutes every night. Ask a friend to make a set of flash cards for different math facts. Take turns quizzing each other.

63. **SHOP 'TIL YOU DROP.** Here's a fun way to review basic math functions. Find an old newspaper with lots of advertisements. Let your shopping fantasies go wild! Imagine that you've been given $10,000 to spend on anything advertised in the paper. What would you buy? A new family car? Stacks of videos? Cut out your "purchases," paste them on a piece of paper, and total them up. Don't forget the sales tax!

64. **PASS THE SLIDE RULE.** Ask a parent or teacher to introduce you to a neighborhood worker who uses math in his or her daily life. This may be an architect (she draws plans to scale), a storekeeper (he makes change for customers), or a scientist (she computes results). Interview the worker to find out all the ways in which he or she uses math in the course of a day. Share your findings with your class. You'll soon realize that math is very much a part of each person's life.

65. **CLEAN YOUR ROOM!** Believe it or not, cleaning your room can lead to higher math skills. That is, if you sort your belongings into categories. Categorizing items, or grouping things according to how they are alike, is one of the building blocks of math. Cleaning your room also has an added benefit—as you clean, you sharpen your organizational skills.

Did you know that mathematicians group numbers into categories such as odd and even numbers, shapes into symmetrical and asymmetrical, and figures into 2-sided, 3-sided, and so on? Next time you organize your room—pairs of socks in this drawer, pairs of shoes in the closet—remember, you're brushing up on your math skills, too.

66. **NO LOAFING HERE.** During spare moments do some mental math. Traveling on a train? Estimate the number of passengers in your car. Is it more than 100? Less than 50? Count the passengers. What is that number's double? Triple? Square root? Did you spot a large bag of popcorn in the cafeteria? How many corn kernels do you think it contains? More than a million? Less?

If you're going on a long drive with your family, take your math book along. Spend some time reviewing areas that are not clear. By the time you arrive at your destination you might not be confused any longer. Make every minute count toward improving your skills.

CHAPTER 10

Special Projects: You're Not Alone

67. VOCABULARY CARDS.

Materials: pack of index cards, pencil, math book.

What to Do: Look through your math textbook for special math words you know, such as *equal* or *divide*. Write each word on one side of the card and the definition, or what it means, on the other. You can also give an illustration.

Example:

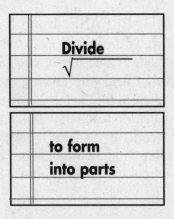

Ask a friend to do the same thing. When you're both finished, exchange cards and study them. As the year goes on, add new words to the pack. Set some time aside every month to test each other.

68. START A BUSINESS. There's a lot of math learning when you open a business. Whether it's a lemonade stand, a baby-sitting club, or a can collection business, you'll learn about investing (where will you get the money to buy the sugar and lemons? How much should you charge for your product to make sure you turn a profit?); setting and totaling hourly rates ("We charged $1.25 an hour. We baby-sat for 4 hours. That will be $5, please"); or making change (a 5-cent deposit on 124 returned cans will yield $6.20).

69. MOVE AHEAD TEN SPACES. Board games are a great way to learn math. Have you ever played *Monopoly* or *Payday*? You can get extra practice in addition and subtraction with games like these. Ask your teacher if some time could be set aside each week to play math games. Think up some new math games, too!

70. PASSWORD, PLEASE. If you have a computer and a modem, you can log on to computer bulletin boards that offer help in a variety of ways. There are areas in these services that deal with solving or studying math problems. You may even find pen pals with whom you can share your problems, or teachers who can help you with your math homework. If you don't have a computer at home but would like to know more about bulletin boards, find out if your school or the local library has a computer center.

71. PHONE FOR HELP. Need help with square roots or averages? Find out if your town or city has a dial-a-teacher service. Some cities, such as New York City, have an afterschool telephone service. Pupils can call a phone number for help with assignments in math and other subjects. Check with your parents before phoning this service.

STUDENT TO STUDENT:

"With a large group of kids, play the game 'Buzz.' To play, sit in a circle. Decide what kind of number you can't say aloud, like all even numbers or any multiple of five. Then, go around the circle, the first player saying 'One,' the next kid saying, 'Two,' and so forth. But when the special number you're not allowed to say comes up, don't say the number, say 'buzz' instead. If you mess up, you're out.

Example: 1, 2, 3, 4, buzz, 6, 7, 8, 9, buzz . . ."

72. **TURN THAT PAGE!** Subscribe to a magazine that's filled with practical ideas for dealing with everyday problems and pastimes, many of them math-related, such as *Zillions: Consumer Reports for Kids*, *Sports Illustrated for Kids*, or *American Girl*. Ask a friend to subscribe to a different magazine and swap with him or her after you've read the latest issue.

73. **21.** If your parents allow it, find out how to play the card game known as 21 and play with a friend. (The object of the game is to get a hand that, when added, comes closest to 21 without going above it.) Not only will you have fun, you'll also sharpen your addition skills.

74. **A FRIENDLY TIP.** The next time you and your folks go to a restaurant, watch what your parents do at the end of the meal. (No, we don't mean if they wipe their mouths with their napkins.) They'll probably look at the bill, then compute a tip, which they leave on the table. Customers often leave a 15% tip. That means they compute 15% of the bill as a special payment to the waiter or waitress. (TIP stands for To Insure Promptness.)

Eating out tonight? Compute the tip yourself. For example, how much tip would you leave for a bill of $42.55? (Possible answer: Take 10% of the total, which is about $4.25, then take another 5% of the bill, about $2.12. Add the $4.25 and $2.12 to get the approximate 15% tip of $6.37. Round off the amount, perhaps leaving $6.30 or $6.50.)

75. **FAMILY MATH.** Volunteer to keep a weeklong math diary for the whole clan. In your notebook, record the family's expenses, from the monthly mortgage payment to the weekly groceries.

Discuss with your family: Where does most of the money go? Is there a way to reduce expenses? Find solutions.

76. **SAVE THE EARTH.** Are you and your friends concerned about the environment? About pollution? Litter? Wasting electricity? Look around your own home or take a walk in your neighborhood. Locate a problem that needs solving and also involves math. (For example, wasting water: Estimate how much water your family uses to wash dishes. Then think of a way to save water. How much do you think you can save in a day? A week? A month? A year?) Write a plan and post it where all can see.

77. **QUILT IT.** Have you read about the quilting bees held during colonial days? Women gathered in bees, social get-togethers in which they worked on one large project. But did you know that making a quilt is also an excellent exercise in math? That's because a quilt requires plenty of measuring and patterning.

Get some friends together. Decide on a design and a size. Plan it first on graph paper. What size will each square be? Nine inches (22.9 cm)? What will the pattern be? Says one seventh grader, an avid quilter: "I once thought math was only numbers! Math is also measuring, planning, and geometry!"

78. THE WINNER IS . . . Ask your teacher to hold a class math fair. Just as a science fair asks kids to tackle science investigations, a math fair has kids explore challenging math problems. To succeed in a math fair you need knowledge, flexibility, patience, and communications skills. You will also need these skills to *plan* the math fair. Ask for volunteers and set aside time after school to plan the events. Allow your committee enough time to write the problems and research the answers. Then prepare the classroom for the math fair. Invite parents if you wish. You can do it!

79. POINT FOR US. Ask your teacher if your class can hold a math bee. Choose one student to be the referee/questioner/scorekeeper, while the other kids choose teams. Have the two teams line up on either side of the room. Played like a spelling bee, the referee asks the first team member a math question. If it's answered correctly, the member wins a point for the team, then goes to the end of the line. The referee then asks the next team member a question, and so on. If answered incorrectly, the member sits down and the first member of the other team gets a question. The team with the most points at the end wins.

80. THE PERFECT GIFT. Create a calendar for the year as a gift for a friend. For each weekday, write an unsolved math problem, such as 97 x 4.5 = ? Have your friend make a calendar with different questions for you. Trade calendars and complete the example for each day. At the end of the year, return the calendars for checking. You'll both get to practice your math skills every day.

81. **LET ME HELP.** Volunteer to help another child, perhaps a younger one, in math. Explaining formulas, discovering problem-solving tricks, and doing drills are good ways to make yourself sharp.

82. **MATH MONTH.** April is Mathematics Education Month (MEM). Ask your teacher to organize special math activities for that month, such as paper-and-pencil projects, outdoor events, computer games, contests, and estimation games that stretch your imagination and your skills!

83. **GET THE KIT.** Ask your school principal, teacher, or department chair to send away for the "World's Largest Math Event" kit. Organized for grade levels K-4, 5-8, and 9-12, the program asks teams of students to complete a math activity around a given task. The kit is available from the National Council of Teachers of Math Headquarters, Dept. I, 1906 Association Drive, Reston, VA 22091-1593. Their fax number is (703) 476-2970.

CHAPTER 11

Test Me!

84. **WHAT'S ON THE TEST?** Make sure you know what topics will be covered on your upcoming test. Will there be questions on subjects covered earlier in the school year? Or will this test only cover the topic recently taught? Check it out before you begin your study sessions to maximize your performance.

85. **TAKE A PRACTICE TEST.** Two nights before a test or quiz, make up some examples that will be covered on the test. If you're studying division with decimals, list five questions that could test your knowledge of that area.

Example: $23.51\overline{)456.90}$

On a separate piece of paper, record your answers. The night before the real test, take the practice test. Which examples did you get right? On which did you make mistakes? Figure out your errors and how to correct them. You may just ace that test!

86. ARE BATTERIES INCLUDED? Ask your teacher what materials you'll be allowed to bring with you on the day of the test. Can you carry a calculator? A list of formulas? Find out ahead of time and show up with the proper materials.

STUDENT TO STUDENT:
"Always check your work, even though you are sure of your answer."

---

87. WHEN'S THE TEST? Hang a calendar above your desk. Fill in the dates of important tests and other special math events. Look at the calendar every day. It's a good way to make sure you have plenty of time to prepare for important exams.

88. TRUST YOURSELF. Your first instincts about an answer to a question on a test are probably right. Don't change an answer unless you have a very good reason to do so.

STUDENT TO STUDENT:
"You should start studying for a math test five days in advance. Study ten minutes a day. Each day study a different concept that will be on the test."

---

89. MULTIPLE CHOICE, ANYONE? Days before your exam, make sure you know what kind of test you're studying for. Is it an open-ended test with more than one solution? Or is it a right-or-wrong exam? The answer to that question will determine how you prepare.

90. 100% OR BUST! Keep track of your progress on tests or quizzes by recording your grades on a chart like the one below. At a glance, you can tell whether or not your grades are going up and by how much.

Reward yourself when your grades soar!

MY MATH PROGRESS							
100							
90							
80							
70							
60							
50							
40							
30							
20							
10							
0							
SEPT.22 QUIZ	SEPT.30 TEST	OCT.10 TEST	OCT.17 QUIZ	OCT.24 TEST	NOV.02 QUIZ	NOV.09 TEST	NOV.14 TEST

91. **CHECK THAT WORK!** When you take an exam, allow some time at the end for checking your work. Go over each example again, making sure your answers are correct. Don't let carelessness lower your grade!

92. **SUBTRACTION CHECK.** Are you completing a page of subtraction examples? You can check if you're right by covering the top number and adding your answer to the number above it. If the sum is the number with which you started, you're correct. (That's because addition is the *inverse*, or opposite, of subtraction.)

Example:
Subtraction

$$\begin{array}{r} 467 \\ - \underline{154} \\ 313 \end{array} \qquad \begin{array}{r} 154 \\ + \underline{313} \\ ? \end{array}$$

> **Always double-check your work by adding up!**

93. **LET'S GET PERSONAL.** Imagine that you're reading a word problem and your mind starts to drift.

Problem:

Bobby works in a toy store. He has 10 boxes of yo-yos. There are 8 yo-yos in each box. How many yo-yos does he have in all?

You might say to yourself, "Who cares about this yo-yo Bobby? I don't know him and I don't care to know about his yo-yos!"

You can make the problem real by substituting names of people in your life. Use the name of your best friend Scott or your favorite movie star. Then read the word problem again. It's more fun to solve problems when you know the people in them!

94. READ, THEN REREAD. Be sure to read a word problem carefully. Read it once, just to get the overall idea. Then reread the problem, thinking carefully about the question. Concentrate. Many good math students read the question several times before working on the answer.

95. **GET THE BIG PICTURE.** Read through the whole test, skimming to get a sense of which problems seem easy, and which may be tough. With a light pencil mark, put an *E* next to all those that seem Easy. Put a light *T* next to those that might be Tough. Go back to the easy ones, and complete them first. Then tackle the others. You'll build your confidence as you answer the easier problems.

96. **WORK AT YOUR OWN PACE.** In every class, there are always a few wise guys who finish the test fast, hand in their papers, then gloat that they're the first ones done. Ignore those kids. Don't let their frantic pace fluster you. Concentrate on your own work, and this will pay off. Says one seventh grade teacher: "I had a pupil in my class who was always the first one done at test time. He finished his paper in record time, then stomped up to my desk, showing off. Problem was," the teacher sighed, "he worked very fast but he also made the most errors. He was not my best math student that year."

97. **LOOK AHEAD.** Keep in mind that the nature of standardized tests is changing. In your parents' day, they may have been simply multiple choice ("How much is 27 x 8? Is it 218? 237? 216? 45?"). Each example may have taken 30 seconds to complete and there was only one right answer.

But nowadays, you and your classmates may get more open-ended standardized exams that require writing. Some examples may take from 15 to 45 minutes to complete! For instance, you may be asked to study a chart, then explain in writing what it means. Or you may be asked to design a game, telling how many players are needed, how many coins are needed, and how many coin tosses make up a turn. Many possible answers are correct!

When you a know a standardized test is coming up, talk to your teacher about the nature of the exam. Then work out a study schedule that will give you plenty of time to review. Remember to include time in your schedule for your other subjects—and for some fun!

CHAPTER 12

Strut Your Stuff

98. **KEEP A MATH PORTFOLIO.** No matter what your grades, you can keep a special folder, called a *portfolio*, that gives "the big picture" of your progress in math. A portfolio shows your best work or most improved work for the year. In it you can display samples of:

- special homework pages
- activity sheets
- projects
- tests
- math certificates or awards
- math reports
- audiotape of you delivering a math report or assignment
- photos of you engaged in a math project

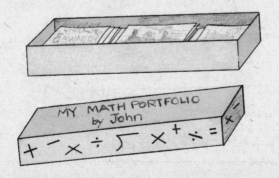

One fourth grader showed this in his portfolio: a diagram of his solution to a geometry problem, some math quizzes, his math goals for the term, two tests, his record of a portfolio conference with the teacher, a math certificate, a photo of him accepting a math award in class.

To whom should you show your portfolio?
- teachers
- parents
- classmates
- possible employers
- other people interested in your math skills

HOW TO MAKE A MATH PORTFOLIO

MATERIALS:
- a clean, empty box with a lid, such as a lingerie box, shoe box, pizza box, or empty board game box. Or, you can use a pocket folder.
  - crayons or markers
  - paste or glue (optional)

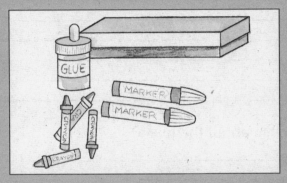

WHAT TO DO: Cover the box (or folder) with your name, the words "My Math Portfolio," and any designs, photographs, or magazine pictures that reveal "who you are" as a math student. Place the portfolio in a safe part of your room, where you know you can always find it.

Save your math work for a few weeks in a separate folder called a work folder. After about eight weeks, pick out special pages or projects that show off your skills and place them in your portfolio. To each piece, attach a note that explains why you selected it. (You can use the *In My Math Portfolio* form on page 86.)

Name _____ Date _____

In My Math Portfolio
_____

(Title of Math Piece)

I chose this for my math portfolio because
_____
_____
_____
_____
_____
_____

I like this about the piece
_____
_____
_____
_____
_____

The piece shows that I can
_____
_____
_____
_____
_____

99. WRITE TO NEXT YEAR'S TEACHER. At the end of the school year, find out who your math teacher will be next year (if you can). Even if it's a teacher you've studied with before, write a letter to that person. Explain to the teacher what your math strengths and goals are for the year. Start off on the right foot!

100. CALCULATE IT! Most people know how to use a calculator. In high school and college, you'll probably be using one in your math and science classes. Now's the time to brush up on your calculator skills. Check your local library for calculator math workbooks or books of calculator games. Or ask to browse through your teacher's library. Learn what a calculator can do for you.

101. NOW HEAR THIS! Inform a friend, a family member, or a classmate that you've read *101 Ways to Boost Your Math Skills*. Tell this person two things you learned by reading the book. As you go through the school year, reread sections of the book to refresh your memory and keep your study habits on track.

Books That Help

Books for Kids

Blum, Raymond. *Mathemagic*. New York: Sterling, 1991.

Brittain, Bill. *All the Money in the World*. New York: Harper Trophy, 1979.

Burns, Marilyn. *The I Hate Mathematics! Book*. New York: Little, Brown, 1975.

Burns, Marilyn. *This Book is About Time*. New York: Little, Brown, 1978.

Coffland, Jack and David A. Coffland. *Football Math: Touchdown—Activities and Projects for Grades 4-8*. Glenview, IL: GoodYear Books (Scott Foresman), 1995.

Cushman, Jean. *Do You Wanna Bet?: Your Chance to Find Out About Probability*. New York: Clarion, 1991.

Javna, John and the EarthWorks Group. *50 Simple Things You Can Do to Save the Earth*. Kansas City, MO: Andrews and McMeel, 1990.

Johnson, Mildred. *How to Solve Word Problems in Algebra: A Solved Problem Approach*. New York: McGraw-Hill, 1976.

Juster, Norton. *The Phantom Tollbooth*. New York: Random House, 1961.

Kimeldorf, Martin. *Creating Portfolios for Success in School, Work, and Life*. Minneapolis, MN: Free Spirit, 1994.

Manes, Stephen. *Make Four Million Dollars by Next Thursday*. New York: Bantam, 1991.

Rockwell, Thomas. *How to Get Fabulously Rich*. New York Dell, 1990.

Workbooks and Kits for Kids

Troll Fun With Math. Grade Four–Grade Six. Mahwah, NJ: Troll Associates, 1995.

Van Der Meer, Ron and Bob Gardner. *The Math Kit*. New York: Charles Scribner's Sons (Macmillan), 1994.

Books for Parents and Teachers

Bolt, Brian. *The Amazing Mathematical Amusement Arcade*. Cambridge, MA: Cambridge University Press, 1984.

Green, Nancy Sokol. *Raising Curious Kids: Over 100 Simple Activities to Develop Your Child's Imagination*. New York: Crown, 1995.

Griffiths, Rachel and Margaret Clyne. *Books You Can Count On: Linking Mathematics and Literature*. Portsmouth, NH: Heineman, 1988.

Muschla, Judith A. and Gary R. Muschla. *The Math Teacher's Book of Lists*. Englewood Cliffs, NJ: Prentice Hall, 1995.

Rafoth, Mary Ann, Linda Leal, and Leonard DeFabo. *Strategies for Learning and Remembering: Study Skills Across the Curriculum*. Washington, DC: National Education Association of the United States, 1993.

Ruedy, Elisabeth and Sue Nirenberg. *Where Do I Put the Decimal Point? How to Conquer Math Anxiety and Let Numbers Work For You*. New York: Avon, 1990.

Ohanian, Susan. *Garbage Pizza, Patchwork Quilts, and Math Magic: Stories About Teachers Who Love to Teach and Children Who Love to Learn.* New York: W. H. Freeman and Company, 1992.

Stenmark, Jean Kerr, Virginia Thompson and Ruth Cossey. *Family Math.* Berkeley, CA: Lawrence Hall of Science, 1986.

Formulas

Area

There are different formulas for calculating the area of different shapes. Use these formulas to calculate the area of some common shapes.

base x height = area of a rectangle/parallelogram/rhombus

base x height ÷ 2 = area of a triangle

$side^2$ = area of a square

π x $radius^2$ = area of a circle

Volume

To find the volume of a shape you must first figure out what the shape is. Then use one of these formulas to calculate the volume.

length x width x height = volume of a cube or a rectangular prism

base x height ÷ 3 - volume of a pyramid/cone

base x height = volume of a cylinder

The volume of a cube can also be calculated by using this formula: $side^3$

Other Formulas

rate x time = distance

π(Pi) = 3.14

Metric Conversion Table

1 inch = 25.4 millimeters
1 inch = 2.54 centimeters
1 foot = 30.48 centimeters
1 yard = .91 meter
1 mile = 1.61 kilometers

1 ounce = 28.35 grams
1 pound = .45 kilogram
1 US ton = .91 metric ton

1 teaspoon = 4.93 milliliters
1 tablespoon = 14.78 milliliters
1 fluid ounce = 29.57 milliliters
1 cup = .24 liter
1 pint = .47 liter
1 quart = .95 liter
1 gallon = 3.79 liters

1 mile per hour = 1.61 kilometers per hour

Conversion from Fahrenheit to Celsius: subtract
32 and then multiply the remainder by $\frac{5}{9}$.

Index

Notes